Father's Day

Blaine Wiseman

Weigl

Published by Weigl Educational Publishers Limited
6325 10th Street S.E.
Calgary, Alberta
T2H 2Z9

www.weigl.com

Library and Archives Canada Cataloguing in Publication data available upon request.
Fax 403-233-7769 for the attention of the Publishing Records department.

ISBN: 978-1-77071-634-6 (hard cover)
ISBN: 978-1-77071-635-3 (soft cover)

Printed in the United States of America in North Mankato, Minnesota
1 2 3 4 5 6 7 8 9 0 14 13 12 11 10

062010
WEP230610

Editor: Josh Skapin
Design: Terry Paulhus

Weigl acknowledges Getty Images as its primary image supplier for this title.
Alamy: page 9.

We gratefully acknowledge the financial support of the Government of Canada through the Canada Book Fund for our publishing activities.

Contents

What is Father's Day?

Father's Day is a time to celebrate fathers. On this day, children spend time with their father. They may take him to a **sporting event** or give him a special gift.

4

When is Father's Day?

In Canada, Father's Day is celebrated on the third Sunday of June each year. Any man who helps care for a child may be celebrated on Father's Day. This includes stepfathers, brothers, grandfathers, and uncles.

6

Father's Day Message

About 4,000 years ago, there was a boy named Elmusu. He lived in a place called Babylonia. Elmusu carved a special message to his father on a card made of **clay**. He wished his father good health and a long life. The tradition of honouring fathers has continued ever since. Today, many children give their fathers cards they make or buy.

Father's Day in North America

The first known Father's Day event in North America took place in 1908. On July 5, a church in West Virginia spent the day honouring men who had died in a recent explosion. Most of the men had been fathers.

10

Father's Day in Spokane

The first official Father's Day was celebrated in Spokane, Washington, on June 19, 1910. Sonora Dodd's mother had died years earlier. She wanted a day to honour fathers who raised their children. Sonora held special events on her father's birthday that year. Soon, people across the United States and Canada began celebrating Father's Day.

Father's Day Traditions

Families celebrate Father's Day in different ways. Some people have picnics with their father. Taking a bike ride or playing a game of golf are other common Father's Day activities.

Father's Day Around the World

Many countries around the world hold similar celebrations. These events are held on different days throughout the year. In Nepal, Father's Day takes place the day after the **full moon** in late August or early September.

16

Father of the Nation

Father's Day is celebrated on the king's birthday in Thailand. This is because the king is called the "Father of the Nation." On this day, children give their father a canna flower.

Celebrating in Germany

In Germany, Father's Day takes place 40 days after Easter. It is a holiday called Ascension Day. Christians believe this is the day that Jesus Christ went to Heaven. Most people have the day off from work or school. Men take part in a hiking trip. They pull a **wagon** filled with traditional foods and drink.

Symbols of Father's Day

On Father's Day, many people wear a rose to honour their father. The colour of the rose has a special meaning. People wear a white rose to honour a father who has died. Those who wear a red rose have a father who is alive.

Glossary

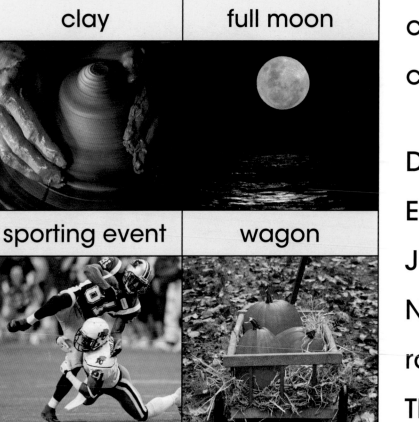

clay	full moon
sporting event	wagon

Index